I0170246

TELL ME MORE

Humor in a Digital Age: Conversations with Scammers, Clerks and Kids

TONY ACREE

ERUDITE
PRESS

ISBN: 978-1-937979-76-8

Cover and illustrations by Katy Acree

Erudite Press

Goshen, Kentucky 40026

www.eruditepress.com

For my grandmother Nanny who taught me laughter always outshines the darkness.

FOREWORD

I've been asked why I mess with scammers. The truth? Several reasons. Mainly, it's to keep my brain active. As a writer of fiction, I worry about ideas drying up. I'm what people call a "pantser," meaning, I write by the seat of my pants. I don't do outlines. I don't plan ahead. Which means when I sit down to create the next Great American Novel, I do it on the fly.

What to do when the fly crashes and burns?

Messing with scammers, creating an alternate reality from scratch, allows me to stretch my creative muscle, making it work hard in a short period of time, keeping the imagination nimble in the process. That's one reason.

Another is if I'm keeping them busy then they aren't scamming someone who might fall for their promises of Facebook cash, IRS refunds, or the newest government grant giveaway. You'd like to think no one falls for this kind of thing, but they do.

I asked one phone scammer pretending to be the IRS, after letting him know I'm a writer, how many people he got to fall for his pitch. Surprisingly he answered. "A good day is ten to fifteen."

When asked how much he averaged bringing in for each one, he responded, "About ten grand." Then he hung up.

The third reason, and the main one, is it's easy. Offer up a little desperation, let them know you are short on cash and their offer of five-hundred grand in special internet winnings is a God send, and you have them. They think they are scamming you, but in truth, you've snagged them.

What follows are several of the conversations I've engaged in on Facebook and Instagram.

In addition, toss in a a few conversations with store clerks and several discussions with my twin girls, Katy and Lauren, and you have *Tell Me More*.

Enjoy.

CHAPTER ONE

There's always a first. And the following conversation is THE one. I've often kept scammers on the phone, when I have the time, and decided to do the same with Facebook scammers. The rest is scammer history. In all scammer conversations, I've left their grammar, punctuation and spelling as is.

Here is an ongoing conversation with a scammer who contacted me pretending to be someone I know. (The fun stuff is more in the second half. I didn't want to lose them too soon.)

Friend's Stolen Name (FSN): Hello How are you doing?

Me: Good. You?

FSN: Am doing great. Hope you have heard about the latest trending going on?

Me: **No. Tell me more!**

FSN: Have you heard about the federal government grant?

Me: I haven't. Tell me more.

FSN: International Monetary Fund is for those who need assistance paying for bills, buying a home, starting their own business, going to school, or even helping raise their children with old and retired people and they are giving everyone that work or not working a grant from $200.000 upward to help all and you can also apply too. Have you heard of Attorney Mark Thomas jr?

Me: Sweet. No, I haven't.

FSN: Have you heard about him he was the one who help me to get my grant and told me that am not to pay it back that's not a loan I can give you her contact to apply as well

(No punctuation and misspellings are consistent red flags with scammers.)

Me: Sign me up.

FSN: Are you ready to contact him now

Me: Sure.

FSN: Okay i will send you his contact now

Me: Yes em. How do I know you're not a scammer?

FSN: This is not a scam. This is real and legit have already gotten my own. Am not a scammer i know you will thanks me when you get yours

Me: Excellent. I trust you.

FSN: called you?

Me: Couldn't hear you.

(They face timed me and I answered and pretended I couldn't hear them.)

FSN: And me too. let me message the attorney maybe his on the site so that i can give you his contact. Do you get that?

Me: Excellent. I can.

FSN: This is his private text number (209) **-**** text her now that you are ready to claim your wining money. And also let him know I refer you okay, do that now and keep me posted on here so I can put you through on how I get mine

Me: I have to pass. I just got an email I owe the IRS. I can't do anything till I get that straightened out.

FSN: Who told you you owe the irs?

Me: I got an email from them. Crap. This sucks. I have a question. You gave me the phone number for a guy, but then said to text "her". If I get the IRS stuff ironed out, I don't want to offend anyone.

FSN: I mad a mistake when typing. I made a mistake

Me: No worries. Is it a guy or gal?

FSN: How much are you paying for the irs. Is a man

Me: They say I owe around 8 grand. A bit over.

FSN: So you need money to pay it now. Hello Me your not replying my message

Me: Sorry. I was driving. I called a friend of mine to meet me for lunch. I am freaking out over the IRS request. I'm going to ask her to loan me the money.

FSN: Hello? Are you there? i need your quick response

Me: I'm here. I respond quickly. Quicker than a speeding bullet.

FSN: How much do you wanna pay for the irs?

Me: I don't want to pay anything. My friend can only afford to lend me $69 of the $8000 needed.

FSN: You know what you can apply for the grant and you will get your money so that you can get pay your irs fee

Me: I like that idea. But I've had another offer since you last contacted me I have to consider.

FSN: You know what contact him now and let me know what is going on?

Me: There is a Nigerian prince looking to hide money in the USA. In exchange for depositing the money, I get to keep part of it. I don't think it's real though. What do you think? Have you ever heard of this?

FSN: Nope have not heard about this

Me: Me either. I don't think it's real. I mean, come on, how would a Nigerian prince get my email address? What would you do?

FSN: Are they the one you receives there mail Are you there ?

Me: One sec.....I'm checking something......I'm so nervous I can barely type....this can't be true..... HOLY FRICKIN HELL. I WON THE KENTUCKY STATE LOTERY!!!!!!!!!!! I bought a ticket for Saturday. I didn't do the whole Powerball, but I matched five numbers and the extra ball and I WON A MILLION

DOLLARS!!! THERE IS NO WAY THIS IS HAPPENING. YOU'VE BROUGHT ME FANTASTIC LUCK!!!!!! Thank you!!!!!!!!!!!!!!!!!!!!!!!!!

FSN: So you don't need the grant again ?

Me: Wouldn't I be greedy getting that too?

FSN: To claim the money you have to pay for it also

Me: I can afford to do that now. How much?

FSN: Alright

Me: As long as it's less than a million dollars. Well....million dollars minus taxes....and a new car....and a banjo. I've always wanted a banjo. And maybe a new trampoline. I love jumping on a trampoline. After that, I'll have plenty of money.

FSN: So you are not contacting the attorney again?

Me: Depends on how much. You know me. In the end, I want what's mine. And what is someone else's. It's Christmas. I want the whole thing. Hell, I want Santa's sleigh. I can afford it. No reindeer though, I hear they have gas problems and I'd hate to be behind them in the sleigh. Let me know where I can send you money for helping.

FSN: Have you contact them now

Me: Oh. And I need to buy fidget spinners for all my friends. I called, but they didn't answer. That's kind of strange. What can I get for you?

FSN: Okay

Me: You've earned it. Have you ever had a gas-powered turtle neck sweater? My mother had a fur sink and she loved it. How much will it cost?

(I love old Steve Martin bits.)

FSN: How much do you mean ? i can't understand you?

Me: Yes. how much will it cost me. I have to plan for the future. I think with the money I'll buy an alpaca farm. I love alpacas. Their fur is incredibly soft.

(At this point, they stopped responding.)

* * *

One day I called Walmart.

Me: Do you have any bark collars?

Clerk: What are those?

Me: They keep dogs from barking.

Clerk: Any idea what department?

Me: Men's clothing?

Clerk: Hold one moment.

(Transfers me to men's clothing.)

Clerk: Men's clothing. How can I help you?

Me: I am looking for bark collars.

Clerk: Never heard of 'em.

Me: They keep dogs from barking.

Clerk: What department?

Me: Women's clothing?

Clerk: I will transfer you.

Me: *sigh*

* * *

I worked for sixteen years as a mailman before I quit to be a stay-at-home dad. One day I stopped to talk to a woman who lived on my route with her partner when the following conversation took place. (I start to pull away and then put on the brakes.)

Me: Sorry. I have another piece of mail.

(I hand her an Out Magazine)

Her: I guess the secret is "out" with you.

Me: Yes. I've know for a while.

Her: Does it bother you?

Me: No. I like women too.

Her: (After a pause, she laughs.) That's kind of funny.

Me: I'm glad you thought so. That was an indoor thought which slipped out.

* * *

One afternoon I was in the fast lane at Kroger when an elderly woman turned and looked into my over half full basket.

Elderly Lady (EL): Do you have 15 items?

Me: No.

EL: Then why are you in this line?

Me: (pointing to the express lane sign) Because of the sign.

EL: But you don't have 15 items. That's clear to see.

Me: Yes, ma'am.

EL: Then why are you in this line?

Me (pointing to the express lane sign) Because of the sign.

(Looking confused, she watched as I put my items on the belt and I watched her as she counted each one.)

EL: Why didn't you say you only had 9 items?

Me: Because that's not what you asked. You asked if I had 15 items. I said no. Kroger's express lane operates on quantity, not volume.

EL: Are you being a Smart Alec?

Me: No, ma'am. I'm being a smart ass. I left "Alec" behind a long time ago.

She shot me a dirty look, paid her bill and left.

Me: (I start to whistle *Cold as Ice* by Foreigner.)

The clerk busts out laughing.

* * *

Picking up our order at the drive through window:

Teen girl: Your total is _____ (it wasn't a small amount)

Me: (I hand her my debit card along with a "POW" sound effect.)

Teen: (Looks at me funny while processing my card. She hands it back to me with a receipt).

Me: Thank you. BAZINGA!

Teen: (Squints at me) What?

Me: It's national sound effects day. I'm adding

sound effects to everything I do until I go to sleep, BOOM!

Teen: (Squints even more, but stays silent.)

Katy: (Leans forward to be seen.) No. We're not aware of any mental illness. This is just the way he is.

Me: KAPOW!

Teen: (Slides the window closed while shaking her head.)

Me: (Looking at Katy, I make PacMan end game sound.)

Katy: *sigh*

* * *

It is the start of another school day.

Lauren: The bus is coming!

Me: No it's not.

Lauren: (Two minutes later.) I hear the bus!

Me: No you don't.

(This goes on for 15 minutes.

Then, until like, the 20th time:)

Lauren: I hear the bus!

Me: Yes, it's your bus.

Lauren: Told you.

Me: *sigh*

* * *

One day I came in to work to find the post office had been robbed. How brilliant were these robbers? Well, they tried to pry open a safe with a screwdriver. (We found the broken part stuck in the safe.) And then they took only one money order out of a drawer (the fake one) and tried to bail a buddy out of jail with it. Needless to say, they were arrested.

The local police didn't fair much better. The robbery took place at midnight during a pouring rain storm. How do we know this? The local cop on duty stopped in to get his mail and heard voices on the other side of the wall. What did he do? He returned to his car, drove to the back of the post office, and seeing nothing? He left. The next morning the Chief of Police was there and the following conversation happened:

Me: You can tell where they went when they came in the window. (The one the officer didn't check.)

Chief: How can you know that?

Me: Their feet were muddy and the longer they walked, the less mud is on the floor. They went to the other window first and pulled the blinds, then to the safe, then to the front counter where they took the money order.

Chief: You can't tell that from the mud.

(I shrugged and went to get everyone coffee. When I returned the Chief was talking to the Postal Inspector who had just arrived on the scene.)

Chief: And you can tell where they walked as there is less mud the further they go.

Me: (Coming around the corner.) Hey Chief.

Chief: (Embarrassed) Hey, Tony.

Postal Inspector: (He notices the Chief's discomfort, but ignores it.) And you're telling me your officer heard voices but didn't investigate?

Chief: Pretty much.

Postal Inspector: Does Barney have to carry his bullets in his pocket?

Chief: *sigh*

* * *

The following occurred while making a Meijer run.

Me: Excuse me, could you tell me if you sell swim goggles?

Clerk: Yes we do.

Me: I don't see them in the sporting goods section.

Clerk: They don't have them there. They are in the gardening section.

Me: Gardening?

Clerk: Yes. In the gardening section.

Me: Because people swim in their gardens?

Clerk: I guess so.

Me: *sigh*

* * *

During my first semester at Murray State I was invited to attend a men's Bible study and the following conversation took place.

Minister: Gentlemen, while you are on campus

you are going to see a lot of attractive women. You should know the Bible says to look at a woman once is fine. To look at her a second time with lust in your heart is a sin. Do you know what you do about this?

I raise my hand and he points to me.

Me: Take a longer first look.

Minister: (shakes his head confused) No. That's not right.

Me: If looking once is safe, then why not look longer?

(Other guys are shaking their heads in agreement with me.)

Minister: No. The point is we sin every day and the answer is to be saved in Christ.

(I raise my hand again but he refuses to call on me.)

Later in the discussion:

Minister: God is omni-PO-tent.

Me: He's also omnipotent.

Minister: He's that too.

For some reason I was never invited back.

* * *

(I sing a song, finishing with Peace Out.)

Lauren: Dad, don't try to be cool. It's embarrassing.

Katy: Yeah dad, people might hear you.

Lesson learned: My twins are old enough now that I can embarrass them in public.

LET THE MAYHEM BEGIN!

* * *

The following conversation took place at the bank:

Teller: How are you?

Me: I've been learning teen slang so I can relate to my twins' friends. Things like "BAE," "fam" and "lit."

Teller: Are you lit right now?

Me: Sister, I'm always lit.

Teller: I don't doubt it.

Me: I can tell you this, because we are fam.

Teller: (shakes her head)

Me: Word up? Foshizzle?

(I get back to the car and relate the use of cool slang in the bank.)

Lauren: You need serious help.

Katy: We can't let you out in public anymore...

* * *

Always wanting to give my kids sound advise:

Me: Never eat a possum sandwich.

Katy: (ewww) Why not?

Me: Because it just lays around. Get it? Lays around? Possum?

Katy: You are so weird.

(Gaylene, you're not the only one that thinks this.)

* * *

I went to the pharmacy to pick up a prescription for my wife. The clerk handed me the meds.

Clerk: Do you have any questions for the pharmacist?

Me: Does he know the winning lottery numbers? Does he know the secret to world peace? Was Paul really the Walrus?

Clerk: (after a three or four second pause) Do you have any other questions for the pharmacist?

Me: Sure. Is Big Foot real? What did the final scene of the Sopranos really mean? Why did my girl-friend dump me in 6th grade?

Clerk: (after an even longer pause) I think I can guess an answer to that last one. Do you have any questions about the medication?

Me: No. I'm good. Thanks.

Clerk: (Shuts the window)

Lesson learned. When the pharmacy asks if you have any questions, they really don't want you to ask them.

* * *

The twins had to draw a picture of what they think is beautiful and then take it to school. The first thing Katy drew was a dollar sign. I am in SO much trouble.

* * *

I had my first "I want to get to know you" scammer. She started asking about my books. She claimed to be from Michigan and living in LA, but didn't know what "howdy" meant and never heard of Amazon. She says her husband died in an accident. Then our conversation transitioned into this and occurred over 4 hours:

Scammer (SC): I don't think I can have someone like Melvin anymore but tired of been lonely

(A hallmark of scammers is poor grammar. I've left their words as they sent them.)

Me: I understand.

SC: That is why I get in touch with you when I'm bored

Me: Ah. I'm an exciting kind of guy. Nonstop party. There are champagne bottles ALL over my house.

SC: Hmm You teasing me or what

Me: Never. I am a man of mystery. Of intrigue. It's all about the tattoos.

SC: I'm a honest and caring woman too but death make me live alone

Me: Women love the fact I am a mountain climber. Or they love taking a trip on my boat. As a bestselling writer, I do well. It's a yacht. Well, almost a cruise ship, but I don't want to brag.

(Not only do I not own a boat, I can't even swim.)

SC: But I believe there is still hope once I haven't gave up

Me: Have you ever seen the show Castle?

SC: Thanks you just make my day

Me: They based the show on me.

(Not true. While my twins think I'm LIKE Castle, and my wife wishes I WAS Castle, and I want to grow up to BE Castle, they have no clue who I am.)

SC: It's been a while I have felt this way before.

I'm getting excited while chatting with you

Me: I'm sure. Most women do. It's the aftershave. Here's a link to a show based on me:

(The link is to Castle season 1 trailer.)

SC: I have to take all my time tonight to read some of your novel I love your work Kind of motivation

Me: You will have to let me know what you think. I spent 3 years on the New York Times best seller list. They paid me to drop off.

(While I am an Amazon bestseller, I've yet to make the NY Times Bestseller list. It's coming.)

SC: Yes that's compulsory

Me: I'm fairly tall. nearly 6 foot 6.

(Actually I'm 5'10", but a man can dream.)

SC: Cool I will like to have a picture from you

Me: Here is a drawing of me when I was younger.

(Victor McCain, the main character in my books, by Kevlen Goodner.)

SC: Baby you have got a talent since you have younger

(I have no clue either what this means.)

Me: I cleaned up well once we shaved off all the extra hair. We used the extra hair to make a shirt.

SC: I love the drawing and I'm saving the picture on computer

Me: Glad you liked it. That same drawing is hanging in the Louvre.

SC: Honey I love hardworking. That is why o don't relent I love that Honey you can text me on my gmail Melissavictoria637@gmail.com I want you to have it

Me: Thanks. That's very nice of you. I will add it to the pile of requests.

SC: OK. What is your plan for the rest of today?

Me: I think I will take a few hours and go save baby seals on the beach. I like to do something to help Mother Earth each day.

SC: Good That's is nice How much time will that take you

Me:I can save about 4 seals an hour. So, maybe two. And you?

SC: I want to do some work in the backyard now

Me: There are a lot of seals on the beaches of the Ohio River. It's a real issue. Enjoy the evening.

(The only seals on the Ohio River are...well...there are none.)

SC: Thanks I hope we can chart later. And I'm wondering why you don't want to have my number.

And you don't want to give your either is there any problems about that

Me: As a bestselling author, women ask for my number ALL the time. I have to be cautious. After what happened the last time I gave it out. Wow. It was something else.

SC: Oh I'm sorry then. You can have it with you

Me: It's quite the story. She was a Russian spy. Can you even believe it? She wanted to recruit me to work with the KGB. They wanted me to write a book about them. They wanted me to ghost write a novel for Putin. When I pointed out I don't speak Russian, they said they'd teach me. I do speak Chinese, however. I order at the local restaurant all the time.

(I say chow mein with the best of them.)

SC: Oh I don't speak any language except English (I don't think she's being completely honest with me.) You have pass through many things/ I will have slot of experience to gain from you

Me: Thanks. I've done a lot of things. There was the time I got the Dali Lama drunk. That's quite a story. He's a real party animal, but comes off all normal.

SC: Lol That funny

Me: Yep. Good thing he had bail money.

SC: Yeah When have you been started writing story

Me: I got stranded in the Sahara Dessert once. I found my way out after making a compass out of a cactus and a bit of camel hair. You have to do it right to get it to work. I wrote my first novel at the age of 12.

(My first novel came out the day before my 50th birthday.)

SC: Wow that sound good

Me: I'm lucky to still be alive

SC: Wow

Me: I own 9 cars. You should see my collection. One is a tank I got from the Maharajah of Cameroon for teaching his daughter how to play a kazoo. He's a riot.

SC: (She spends more time begging for my number.)

Me: Sorry, Melissa. The supermodel who got it the last time made it rough. She kept drunk texting me about Taylor Swift and wanting me to join them in the Bahama's. I was too busy hanging with Brad Pitt and drunk texting Angelina Jolie.

SC: Did you write the Gmail I give you down

Me: I wrote it on my arm in non-erasable marker. I think Taylor Swift is going to be #%@% off. She wrote THREE songs about me.

Me: I have to go. Brad Pitt is picking me up and I have to go save those seals. I hope you enjoy the book.

* * *

The twins and I were at Great Clips hair salon when the stylist asked about my next project. I told her I was writing a fantasy novel for my daughters who are into dragons.

Stylist: Oh, I bet they love zombies, too.

Lauren: No, we love the mythical, not the supernatural.

Me: How old are you?

(I'm stealing her quote, by the way.)

* * *

Raising twin girls can have its moments.

Lauren: A boy wants to be my boyfriend, but I said no because he is too young for me.

Me: How old is he?

Lauren: 7.

Me: You're only 8.

Lauren: Yes, but I'm turning 9 and I don't think it would've worked out, because I'm so much older.

Me: *sigh*

* * *

After listening to Diamond Rio's *One More Day* about a man wishing for one more day with the woman he loved, the following conversation took place:

Katy: You know what I would wish for?

Me: What?

Katy: I'd wish for my family and friends to be able to live together in happiness forever.

Me: That's sweet.

Katy: What about you? What would you use your one wish on?

Me: Pennies.

Katy: (Puzzled look.) Pennies?

Me: Yep. I'd do away with pennies.

Katy: (Throws her hands up in the air.) Why would you want to do that?

Me: Because I get tired of rolling them. People should have to round up or round down and it would make accounting easier. Then we wouldn't need pennies.

Katy: Pennies.

Me: Yep.

Katy: *sigh*

* * *

After I fixed lunch one autumn day, the twins had the nerve to ask me what I had for dessert—with two huge bowls of Halloween candy still left on the table. As they explained to me, quite rationally, THAT was Halloween candy—NOT regular lunch dessert and they shouldn't be forced to use their own candy for what we normally give them for "free." Ahem. *sigh*

* * *

Christmas was approaching and I took the twins shopping to find gifts for their cousins.

Lauren: Dad, Toys R Us is a dream for kids!

Me: Lauren, the smile on your face is the dream for dads.

(Take that Santa!)

* * *

When the twins were young, my wife traveled a lot for business. One day we were on the way back from my mother's house and the twins were watching Bambi on the car DVD player. We got to the point where the hunter shoots Bambi's mom when this conversation took place:

Lauren: What happened to Bambi's mom?

Me: She's gone, pumpkin.

Katy: (long pause) Ohhh...She's on a business trip.

Me: Good call.

* * *

And another conversation with the twins:

Katy: What year were you born?

Me: 1963

Lauren: You must have dressed really different back then.

Me. Yep. I wore diapers.

Twins: (Long stare, then they both shake their heads.)

* * *

I went to the Kroger Pharmacy to pick up a prescription for my wife on the 9th of the month. I told the clerk I had a pickup and gave the clerk my name.

Me: I'm here to pick up my wife's prescription.

Clerk: We could not fill it as she is out of refills until next month.

Me: When was it last filled?

Clerk: On the 9th. (Of previous month.)

Me: What's today?

Clerk: The 9th.

Me: Does this suggest anything to you?

Clerk: Yes, she is out of refills.

Me: Could I speak to the pharmacist please?

Clerk: Sure.

(She goes to get the pharmacist, I tell him I'm here to pick up a prescription and give him my name. He goes over to the bin and gets me the prescription.)

Clerk: Huh. I thought they were out of refills.

* * *

One afternoon, Katy and I blew by a Lamborghini on River Road in my Nissan Rogue. The man looked my way with shock and dismay. I returned the look with dispassionate arrogance.

My only regret was not having any Grey Poupon.

Then, after telling my daughter Lauren this story, we were back on the road. This time we passed a Corvette.

With the window down, Lauren yelled to the driver, "Do you have any grey mustard?"

* * *

I went to the Oreck store to buy vacuum bags. As it happens, they come in their own bag. The following conversation is almost verbatim.

Clerk: Would you like me to put your bags in a bag?

Me: Sure. While you're at it, can you give me change for my change? (I hand her a quarter.)

Clerk: Sure. (She hands me two dimes and a nickel.)

Me: Could you also give me a receipt for my receipt?

Clerk: Absolutely. (She then writes up another receipt).

Clerk: As she hands it to me she asks, "Are you an English professor?"

(At the time I was a stay at home dad, but had delivered mail for 16 years.)

Me: That's the number two guess when people try and guess what I do, right behind garbage collector and right ahead of astronaut.

Clerk: I knew it!

I walked out with my bags in a bag, my change for my change and a receipt for my receipt.

* * *

Katy pointed to a scar on my arm.

Katy: Where'd you get that one?

Me: Knife fight when I was younger.

Katy: (Eyes wide.) Tell me about it.

Me: I was walking down a dark street, late at night, when a I was attacked. The blade sliced across my arm, but I caught the attacker with a back-hand blow and then a smash with my forearm ending the fight.

Katy: (In awe.) Wow.

Wife: (My wife walked by and saw us looking at the scar and stops.) Showing her the scar from when you were playing with the cat?

Katy: (Gives me an exasperated almost teenage look.)

Me to Katy: It was a dangerous cat.

* * *

A new one for me. An Instagram scammer. Who knew they existed?

Bill: Hi, Good day to you and your entire household. Hope you have fair weather condition today.

Me: It's snowing. I wouldn't go to a fair today.

Bill: I'm Bill....From US. CEO of ******* International and you?

(There is a guy named Bill who is the CEO of *******. I think this Bill is pulling my leg.)

Me: I'm a writer. I write things.

Bill: What's your name please?

Me: Rupert. How can I help you Bill?

Bill: Where is your current location?

Me: In my house.

Bill: Where are your place of home?

Me: Kentucky.

Bill: Are you married?

Me: I'm not sure you're my type.

Bill: what do you mean Me?

(I guess he didn't like my alias Rupert.)

Me: You're asking if I'm married...

Bill: yeah is that a bad really you Me? (You would think an American CEO would use better grammar.)

Me: I have the whole world in my hands. Someone should write a song about that.

Bill: do you have kids?

Me: Define kids?

Bill: I don't understand?

Me: Why all the questions Bill? Are you practicing to be a Census Taker?

Bill: I have something to discuss with you but before I would perceive I will like to know more about you

Me: Yes, but how can I tell if I want to tell you stuff that I don't know what you're telling me, truth be told.

(I thought I'd try non-sensical to see if he noticed. Guess not.)

Bill: yeah but I will like to know more about you Me

Me: I have to keep some secrets. Why spoil the mystery? Some people think I'm an enigma wrapped in a question. Actually, most people just question me.

Bill: can we proceed?

Me: By all means, Bill. Lead the procession.

Bill: I am writing following the information about you and your surname on the international web directory. I hope you are capable and reliable champion this business opportunity.

Me: I have the strength of 10 men. Hear me roar.

Bill: I have in my banking system the existence of a huge amount of value add 7,500,000 of money that belongs to a late customer, Mr. Rodney, He was among the death victims in the Malaysian Airlines flight 370 One 8 March 2014. He was unmarried and no children

Me: That is incredibly sad. It's not the fall but the sudden stop that gets you every time.

Bill: the fund is now without any claim because no next of kin was mentioned by Mr. Rodney open an account with our bank so I want to present you with next of kin and benefactor to attend the fun and we share 50-50

Me: Do I have to fly on a plane to get it? Doesn't sound like a good idea. I once flew to Lima Ohio with a clown. I wonder if there were clowns on his flight.

Bill: you have to partner with me and when this victory. You have to also do what I asked you to do!!!

Me: I'm great at following directions. I always win Simon Says.

Bill: I need your immediate response of interest to enable us proceed. Also I can send you the documents backing it up.

Me: How immediate? I'm typing pretty fast as it is. I studied typing.

Bill: well this is a business transaction which has to in your surname a country I need your partnership and I know you will treat this business with maturity

Me: You can count on me. I'm so mature I have an AARP card and I yell at kids to stay off my lawn. Quite mature. I even take Metamucil.

(He sends me a heart emoji. I think he likes me.)

Bill: Are you interested in becoming my business partner?

Me: I think we will make great partners. Like Dean Martin and Jerry Lewis, George Burns and Gracie Allen, Bonnie and Clyde.

Bill: this transaction is top-secret please I don't

when the transaction be exposed, I don't want my coworkers here at standard chartered Bank to know more about this.

Me: No worries. I am an ex Secret Service agent. I have lifelong top-secret clearance despite what happened in Singapore. Don't get me started on that one. I was cleared of all wrongdoing. I can use this money.

Bill: I am happy you accepted my offer of 50-50 is fair. This transaction is 100% risk-free once you follow my instructions.

(He never even paused when I told him I was a secret service agent. This guy has @%$# of steel.)

Me: Sweet. I don't have to dress up to get the money, do I? That is what got me in trouble in Singapore.

Bill: All I have to do is place your name in the bank database as Next of Kin, and as the managing director, I then witness as well to the fund.

Me: Excellent. We were with the president in Singapore at his daughter's birthday party. We all had to dress up as clowns so we would blend in. His daughter got really mad at me because she thought I was a scary clown and they almost shot me, how terrible is that? It almost cost me my job.

(I mention clowns often in my posts and I have no clue why.)

Bill: No you do not have to dress in that matter. Presenting you as the next of kin to the late Mr. Romney is an easy task for me. All I need from you is sincerity and trust that you will not betray me that you're going to see the money on your personal bank account.

Me: Good. Do you like clowns?

Bill: Sure I do. (finally, a scammer who likes clowns) I will present you as a relation to Mr. Rodney and you will show your Identification. No more than 7 days.

Me: Excellent. I'm going to move far away from here. Can I come stay with you, partner?

Bill: Yes, but I'll meet you for the sharing before we come back to my place.

Me: Can I bring my pet?

Bill: Yes. I need the following, Full Name, Date of Birth, Occupation, Contact Address, Phone Number, Marital Status, Photograph or Scanned Copy of Identity Card, Clear Photo of your Face, Email Address

Me: You have to have a photo? The clown makeup left me scarred and I don't look so good. It's why they let me go. My Name is Victor McCain, I was born 12 25 1972, I am currently a bounty hunter, I live at the Derby City Mission in the back room. My email address is TheDevilMadeMeDoIt@gmail.com (all things from my books)

Bill: Occupation?

Me: I track down bail jumpers. And I hand out Old Testament Justice to evil people for God.

Bill: Picture?

(I send another drawing of Victor McCain by Kevlen Goodner.)

Bill: Oh that's a nice one. Address?

    Me: Derby City Mission, Louisville KY 40241

    Bill: Marital status, ID, Phone number?

    Me: I'm single. I had to... Shot my last lover in the hip. She was possessed by a fallen Angel. I know that sounds crazy but it's true. I'll have to get a friend, Kurt Pervis, to scan the docs. (More things from my books.)

Bill: That's OK. You can use your phone camera to scan the docs.

Me: I will have to get Kurt to do that for me. My phone does not have a camera.

Bill: Better I have it right away so I can proceed with your information.

Me: How do I know you don't just want my picture to send it across the Internet? There are people looking for me and I don't want them to find me.

Bill: Not at all, my dear, I guarantee 100% confidentiality. (I think Bill has fallen for me.)

Me: OK. I'll get back to you. I got a call on my other phone and I have to go "take someone out" if you know what I mean.

(I finally needed to stop to go pick up Katy. He/she never gave up. I'll give the individual credit. Instagram scammers are tough. When I got back to my computer, the account was suspended.)

* * *

While at the check-out line at my local Kroger:

Clerk: Nobody likes the metric system. (Looks at me.) Do you like it?

Me: Yes I do.

Clerk: Really?

Me: Yes, ten times over.

Clerk: (stares at me a moment) Oh. Funny.

Me: *sigh*

* * *

I was playing a Trace Adkins song *Ladies Love Country Boys* when I picked up the twins. Katy said the song was right because I was a country boy and she loved me. You can't top that.

* * *

Watching a rerun of Castle over dinner:

Katy: Dad, you are just like Castle.

Lauren: You really are. Except you're older.

Katy: And not as rich.

Lauren: And don't drive as nice a car.

Katy: Or sell as many books. But other than that, you guys are the same.

Me: (Thinking, *"My girls said I was Castle. Sweet!"*) I am ruggedly handsome, aren't I? (Famous Castle line.)

Twins, at the same time: NO.

Me: *sigh*

* * *

I went to Office Depot to buy an ink jet cartridge. I was walking out of the store when a clerk chased me down.

Clerk: Sir, you forgot this.

(He tries to hand me a power cord from a laptop.)

Me: It's not mine.

Clerk: It goes with your purchase.

Me: (I hand him the ink jet cartridge.) Where does it plug in?

Clerk: Didn't you just buy a laptop?

Me: Nope.

Clerk: Are you sure?

Me: You're asking me if I just bought a laptop, then walked out of the store forgetting I had just bought one?

Clerk: Yeah, I guess.

Me: One of us is wrong. Guess which one?

Clerk: I guess we'll just keep it then.

(He turned around shaking his head and goes back in the store.)

* * *

This kind of conversation happened a lot talking to the twins.

Katy: I feel hungry.

Me: (After rubbing her head) Nope. You feel normal.

Katy: You know you're nuts, right?

Me: I take after my daughters.

Katy: True that.

(Who says this—let alone an 8 year old?)

Katy: (After a moments pause) I feel hungry.

Me: (After rubbing her head again.) Nope. You feel normal.

Katy: *sigh*

* * *

Another scammer stole the ID of a friend on Face-Book. The following conversation took place. I changed their name to Stolen Friend FB ID to protect their identity:

Facebook Friend: Hello

Me: Hi, Stolen Friend FB ID

FBF: I notice I can't send msg to all my fb friends

that why I had to set up a fb messenger because i got a virus with my old account hope seeing my request did not bothered you?

Me: Nope. Welcome back.

FBF: Have you heard about the SBG (Small Business Grants) Bonus Program by Facebook? who help hearing ,deaf, retired and some other Facebook users?

(While I'm not deaf, or retired, I am "hearing" and I do qualify as "other" Facebook users.)

Me: **No. Tell me more.**

FBF: The promotion was made to some Facebook user in other to benefit from them its a randomly picked of profile on Facebook $200,000.00 did you get yours from them??? UPS delivered the money to my door step. I saw your name on the list with the shipping company agent, I'm so serious about this i really got the money and it is real and legit did you mean you haven't gotten yours yet??

Me: I sure as hell did not!!! I've been ripped off!!!

FBF: I am telling you the truth. this is real and my bank confirm it. i cant lie to you or mess up with you, so you really have to believe in me. OH MY GOD! I'm not kidding or pulling your legs. [She was not happy pulling one leg.] I saw your name among the Lucky winners when the UPS came down to my door step to deliver my winning money to me. Anyway, i think you should contact the Claiming Agent in charge to claim your own winning. Do you know how to do that?

Me: I don't. But when I find out who stole my

money I'm going to %*¥# them up. You know what I did to that other guy.

FBF: Send a text message to # (575) 347-1855 her name is Agent Carolyn Chamber and tell her that you want to claim your winning money now. Do that right now

Me: How quick can I get the money? My trial lawyer is after me to pay his bill after getting me off the last charge.

FBF: You will got it tomorrow if you follow her instruction., i am assuring you that you will got your winning money tomorrow and have you send her a text message now?

Me: Sweet. The best thing? Now that they found me innocent they can't retry me. How cool is that. Suckers never knew I actually did it. Do you want a finder's fee?

FBF: No.. And have you send her a text message that you want to claim your winning money now?

Me: I will shortly. Texting my lawyer. How come you don't want any? You took a cut of my bank job. I'll keep that on the low down. Just between us. Hey. If I want to keep this from the IRS will you help me hide part of the 200 thousand?

FBF: Yes i will. I am so happy for you

Me: I can't have it show up in my account. The cops are all up in my stuff. Think they can send it to you? And you can pay me as I need it?

FBF: make sure you follow her instructions and

do whatever she told you so that you can got your winning money tomorrow. okay. text her now

Me: I'm texting now. I may need 10 grand to get out of the country. Thc lawyer says the cops are now charging me for fighting in that duel where I nearly killed that guy. Dueling is illegal in Kentucky. Go figure.

FBF: Agent Carolyn Chambers will surely help you out. trust me for that

Me: Sweet.

FBF: i hope you have text her

Me: Hmm. I think the number you gave me is wrong. I got a reply saying it wasn't a cell for Chambers but for a guy named Rupert who runs a ballerina/massage school. (Rupert returns.)

FBF: Sure you got the right number?

Me: That sounds wrong. Are you trying to scam me??? I ain't no freakin ballerina.

FBF: No

OMG

what is going on?

Me: (575) ***-****?

FBF: i am not the kind of person that will lie to you or mess up with you. you really have to believe me and trust in GOD (Obviously this scammer is an atheist. Can you imagine a scammer getting to the Pearly Gates and finding out once they walk in they went straight to Hell?) I am so sad now that you dont trust me

Me: It seems they train ballerinas to give

massages in their spare time. Is the number right??? I WANT MY MONEY!!!

FBF: Yes +1 575-**-****I told you that you should send her a text message

Dont call her. she is always busy with alot of winners. send her a text message

Me: I texted the last time. I might consider being a ballerina if I don't have to wear the outfit. 200 grand would buy a lot of lessons. But don't tell anyone I'm considering doing that. Do you hear me? No one.

FBF: what is your cell number. i will give it to her to text you

Me: You know what I do to people who tick me off. Like that dude in Lima Ohio. They never found him. I buried him along with his unicycle and clown outfit. I hate clowns.

FBF: Trust me

Me: I appreciate you keeping that quiet. And I'll NEVER snitch on you for your sports book gambling. You scratch my back and I'll scratch yours.

FBF: https://www.facebook.com/carolyn.********* click on it and message her

Me: I AM IN DEEP TROUBLE!!! Did you tell someone I was here? Did you turn me in???

FBF: what happen?

Me: I'm in my bedroom and someone kicked in the front door. I'm hiding in the back of my closet. I'm lying behind that stack of Classic Trivial Pursuit games I collected. DID YOU TELL SOMEONE I WAS HERE???? WHY DID YOU DO THAT????

FBF: no i dot i dont did you got a message from Carolyn chamber from facebook

Me: I have to not type for a moment.... they're in the bedroom and they might hear me. Give me a second. It might be the pizza guy. I owe him money too. I'm starting to think you're the cops and you're trying to keep me here so you can arrest me.

FBF: I cant trust me (I wouldn't be too sure of that if I were you.)

Me: If this really is Stolen Friend FB ID, and you turned me in, I will find you. You know this. And if I do, I'll use the same Nerf Gun on you I used on Willard. It won't be pretty. If you think what I do to clowns is bad...I can't trust me? You actually are telling me I can't trust you?

It was at this point they blocked me...

* * *

On the drive back from seeing the eclipse in Tennessee, a drive which took nine hours:

Katy: Lauren you have to try to get some sleep while in the car. We have school in the morning.

Me: (I looked at Katy.) Way to go mom. (She is always looking after others.)

Katy: Someone in this car has to act responsibly.

Me: Whatever. (Pause, then to Katy.) Hey, pull my finger.

Katy: *sigh*

* * *

Overheard:

"There was no pizza because everyone ate it before anyone could get any."

* * *

One afternoon after school:

Lauren: Dad, can you help me with my homework?

Me: Sure, what do you need pumpkin?

Lauren: I need to come up with a slogan to promote a monarchy.

Me: Kings rule, subjects drool!

Lauren: (Stares at me a moment.) I think you prove the point.

Me: Truth in advertising.

* * *

Facebook scammers may be wise to me, but Instagram scammers? Not so much.

Scammer: Hello. Are you there?

Me: Yes. How are you?

Scammer: Am Fine and you?

Me: Living the dream, dreaming to live.

Scammer: That nice. I'm Jason Moore from Facebook social Inc. I was authorized by Facebook promotion board to get in touch with you.

(And doing so on Instagram? Perhaps he forgot where he was.)

Me: Howdy, I am Wilbur from Lagrange. Sweet! I love promotions.

Scammer: I contacted you because I have good news from the Facebook promotion board

Me: **Tell me more.**

Scammer: before I proceed I would love to know if you have been informed about your winnings from any of the other Facebook coordinators?

Me: NO!!! I'm a winner???

Scammer: LOL

Me: Seriously. This is great timing.

Scammer: I'm pleased to inform you of the release the recent results held by Facebook group Promotion.

Me: And I won? I got talked into investing into a clinic and I lost a ton of money. Thank goodness. I am tired of eating spam and drinking Ripple.

Scammer: we embarked on a worldwide promotion and you were randomly selected by your email accounts used on the Internet. Consequent upon this your Facebook profile account was picked as a category a winner.

Me: Woot!!! The clinic was for helping depressed circus clowns, magicians and rodeo clowns. We only had two people show up. How do I get my money? I live near the rodeo circuit and I used to compete.

Scammer: the online draw was conducted by random selection process in unit one $500,000. There were 20 winners this year.

Me: I might be able to get back into the Shetland pony wrangling game. What do I do? I am semi-retired after my accident.

Scammer: your winning is 100% real and legitimate

Me: Dude I believe you. How quick can I be paid? I have the payment coming due on my new car. have you seen the pictures? I took a hearse and turned it into a convertible.

Scammer: are you ready to claim your winnings???

Me: I bought it cheap from the rodeo funeral home. Yes, I am!

Scammer: what I need from you as the following details.

Full Name, home address, email address and mobile number.

Me: We use the car for cowboy funerals. It allows their horse to be tied up to the bumper.

Scammer: Full Name, home address, email address and mobile number.

Me: Jason do I need to pay you a cut? Percentage?

Scammer: I don't mean percentage point in my job

Me: I'm happy to do so. One second. I got a call. (pause) Geez. This guy won't leave me alone. Do you like clowns? He's a former rodeo clown.

Scammer: Yeah

Me: Help a guy once and this is what you get.

Scammer: Can I get your details?

Me: Sure. I'm about 5'6" tall with brown hair and blue eyes. I like piña colada's in the rain, I like to sit at home and watch Netflix. My favorite author is Agatha Christie. Oh, and I hate snoring. Those details?

Scammer: Full Name, home address, email address and mobile number.

Me: You guys will not sell my details, will you?

Scammer: no

Me: Fantastic. The last group sold my name to a mailing list for people who like slinky's. You should've seen the weird mail I got.

Scammer: That was not okay for them to do that

Me: I will get back to you shortly I am picking up my quadruplets at the school. You should try to get five kids in the same car with all their book bags. Chaos. And they eat a ton.

Scammer: OK

Me: Jason when you help me figure out how to invest my money. Will you help me figure out how to invest it?

Scammer: spend your winnings anyway you want okay?

Me: I used to keep my money in cash in my mattress. But then I got bedbugs and the exterminator people found it. It was not pretty.

Scammer: I'm only here to give you your winnings.

Me: That is a bummer. I seem to always lose money. I do not invest very wisely. Like the time I bought shares in a tanzanite mine, but it was not in Tanzania. That was stupid. What details do you need?

Scammer: Full Name, home address, email address and mobile number.

Me: Thank you. I hit my head really hard about a year ago. I don't always remember where I am or what I'm doing.

Scammer: I am asking you for details. Are you joking with me?

Me: You think a head injury is a laughing matter??? Not funny. I'm not happy dude.

Scammer: Sorry about that okay?

Me: I spent nearly a month thinking I WAS a circus clown. And I don't even own an outfit. That's why I bought into the clinic. When I said we only had two customers, one of them was me. The other one ended up being the doctor.

Scammer: I only want to transfer you the winnings.

Me: Have you ever heard of the Kentucky Colonels? It's an honorary society that I belong to. Because you are helping me out I'm going to nominate you to be a member. How cool is that?

Scammer: No problem.

Me: Fantastic! All I need is your street address, email address and cell phone number. You get a lot of great discounts.

(At this point, he quit responding. His loss. Being a Kentucky Colonel is sweet!)

* * *

At a PNC bank (not my home PNC) where they have an award for being a Level 6 Sigma branch.

Me: (To the PNC greeter) I see you are a level six Sigma award winner. How many levels are there?

Greeter: There are six.

Me: Thank you. I needed the context. After all, if there are only six levels then you guys are doing a great job. But if there are 423 levels then not so much. And I would wonder why you're bragging. Good for you guys!

Greeter: (Just smiles)

Me: (Stands and nods)

Greeter: (Continues to try and smile, but it's slipping)

I get that a lot.

While putting away the groceries, my wife yells out to me:

Wife: You bought the wrong lunchables for Lauren.

Me: Didn't you tell me to buy the Pepperoni Pizza Lunchables?

Wife: Yes.

Me: Isn't that what I bought?

Wife: Yes. But the wrong ones.

Me: So I bought what you asked me to buy, but I bought the wrong ones?

Wife: Yes.

Me: *sigh*

* * *

When I went back to the store to buy Pepperoni Lunchables for Lauren (see previous post) there was a clerk staking up Gain Laundry detergent.

Me: I see you're making gains at work today.

Clerk: What?

Me: Gains, you're making gains at work today.

(I know the joke is way LAME, so sue me.)

Clerk: I don't get it.

Me: Never mind, will you just hand me some GAIN detergent?

Clerk: Sure.

Me: *sigh*

* * *

At lunch, after giving the twins grief over using their phones while we eat, I pick up mine to read an email.

Lauren: See. You're doing it.

Me: I'm looking up the egg question for you.

Katy: Egg question?

Me: The Chinese have figured out which came first, the chicken or the egg.

Lauren: And that helps us how?

Me: Isn't this one of the questions that keeps you up at night?

Both girls: NO!

(I finish reading and put my phone down.)

Both girls: Well?

Me: I don't know. I can't read Chinese.

Lauren: (After a long stare she looks at Katy.) And he still managed to get married.

Katy: I know, right?

Me: *sigh*

* * *

I had the local Kroger bakery make my twin girls a cake. I stopped by and picked it up and was on the way to the checkout lane when one of the clerks who knows the twins and me well, asked who the cake was for.

Me: The twins.

Clerk: Both of them?

Me: No, only the good one. I'm making the other one wait a month and won't let her have any presents until then.

Clerk: That'll teach her!

* * *

Just so clerks who are reading this know I'm not picking on them, us regular folks are not much better. I was at a community event and they had a blood donor booth. I give blood regularly and decided to donate while there. When finished, I was standing next to the snack table, gauze around my arm, wearing an "I Just Gave Blood" sticker, when a man walked up.

Man: Did you just give blood?

Me: Nope. I just got some.

Man: Good for you! (He nods and walks off.)

I didn't have time to ask if he worked as a clerk.

* * *

I was talking to a lady about the Great Steam Boat race, held every year the Wednesday before the Kentucky Derby.

Lady: What do steam boats run on?

Me: Hmm. Steam? (I know modern ones mostly do not.)

Lady: That's good to know.

Me: *sigh*

* * *

Me: *"There are three kinds of men. The ones that learn by readin'. The few who learn by observation. The rest of them have to pee on the electric fence for themselves."* - Will Rogers. After reading this quote to my twin girls, they respond:

Twins: What's wrong with you?

Me: That is a long debated question. The jury is still out.

Twins: Somebody needs to find out.

* * *

Can you remember the dumbest thing you ever said?

I can. As teen, I was working at Long John Silvers and the upcoming Friday was Friday the 13th. The following conversation took place between me and the assistant manager:

Me: I wonder if Friday the 13th and Halloween has ever fallen on the same day.

(The moment I say it, I realize how dumb it was. Thankfully, the assistant manager came to my rescue.)

A.M.: I think it has.

Me. No. It hasn't.

A.M.: Yes It has. I'm positive it has.

Me: Nope. And I can prove it.

A.M.: How?

Me: Friday the 13th. What day is Halloween on?

A.M. (Thinks for a moment.) Oh.

Me: *sigh*

* * *

Watching Castle with my twins.

Katy: Dad, you're just like Castle. You're both writers. You're both funny. The only difference is he's rich and you're not. You need to work on that.

Lauren: Yeah, I'd like a Ferrari.

Katy: And I'd like a big tree house.

Lauren: And I'd like---

Me: You know, you two are almost old enough to get jobs.

Both girls: Never mind.

* * *

You'd think the scammers would know me by now. Guess not. Below, FF stands for Facebook Friend.

FF: Hello How are you doing

Me: Doing great. You?

FF: I'm doing great and excited Hope you watch the Fox news lately?

Me: Not lately.

FF: I'm just wondering if you have had anything about the federal government 2018 new year grant

Me: **No. Tell me more.**

FF: The promotion was made by federal government grant in other to benefit from them it is a randomly picked of profile on Facebook

Me: Sweet. How much???

FF: This is specifically place for those who need assistance paying for bills, buying a home, starting their own business, going to school. Even helping raise their children with old and retired people

Me: I'm in desperate need of money with my factory failing.

FF: This is a new program. Did you get yours from them yet?

Me: I opened that place to make socks for pets. And it's not going well. No. I didn't.

FF: OMG.. you mean you have not get your delivery down to you yet.. Do you know how to get in touch with them

Me: Remember the Snake Snuggy? That was my

idea. The problem is since they're cold-blooded, several of them died when they got too warm. Go figure. No, I don't and now I'm panicked.

FF: Oh I get my cash already and five of my friends got the cash too

Me: Another lady bought our socks for her Doberman and he took off running in the house and slid off a back deck. She's suing us. I need cash quick.

FF: You can still get the money too because I saw your name and your profile pics on there winners list when the claim agent and the Fedex manager came to my house to deliver me my cash

Me: Sweet!!!! I've got a new idea and I need cash fast. Starbucks for animals. If people are willing to spend 6 dollars on a latte, I bet they'll spend 3 dollars on a frappuccino for their poodle. What do you think? And they deliver?

FF: All you need to do is to contact the federal government grant office ® desk agent online via (+12532******), You can also Email them on Herick-smith385@gmail.com

They we tell you what to do and the guide lines to get your grant money ok You really need to contact them right now and talk with there claim agent about this grant money OK

Me: Sweet. Thanks for the heads up. I was thinking a tag line like, *"Think of your pooch order them a latte hooch."* Catchy, don't you think?

FF: That's cool.

Me: Any idea how much money? I need at least

100,000. I've found a store location in a warehouse district, next to a rubber plant, not too far from the nuclear power plant. They say if you get close enough, you don't even need to pay for electricity because the whole place glows. Saves on utility bills.

FF: I got sum of $60,000 deliver to me cash, i was so surprise that I got the money deliver to me cash at my door step

Me: But if it's not at least a hundred grand, I'm out of luck.

FF: Wow that's so cool, So just text the claiming agent now and let them know you are ready to claim your grant money Ok

Me: The Snake Snuggy lawsuit is costing me a fortune. Did you ever see our commercials? I thought they rocked. Not only did some of them die, others just wiggled out. Owners never put the harnesses on right. Duh. Several got bit putting on the socks. They come with a disclaimer: "Put on the sock while keeping fingers away from fangs." Some people don't read.

FF: That's the amount I can afford to pay for the shipping money because there is a lot of grant price

Me: One sec. I have to get the kids up.

FF: So you have to text them and know what's going on with your grant money Ok

I'm very serious about this grant money because have already got mine claim from them and this is real and legit OK

Me: Thanks. I'm back. I was telling my kids and

they are SOOOOO excited. They want me to take them to Disney World if there is any money left over, think there will be? I don't want to take them to the one in Florida though. The lines there are too long. There's one in Syria, but you have to sign a waiver about not suing if you get shot or hit with a chemical weapon. Think it would still be safe enough? I hear there are NO lines. How cool would that be? Ride Space Mountain Syria with no lines?

FF: Oh nope you don't have to inform anybody even your family until you get the money deliver to you, so you we just make it a surprise package OK

Me: Well, Hell. You didn't tell me that!!!

FF: It's okay Have you text them yet?

Me: I told my girls. And they texted their friends. And one of their friend's other friends is a Secret Service agent for the president. I figured if he knew about it, we might get our money faster. I'm going to in just a minute. I'm trying to tell one of our pet socks customers how to get booties on a Siamese Cat. She puts them on, and then when the cat licks its paws, it gets stuck to their tongue. The material we use is really not all that comfortable.

FF: I told you not to inform anyone about this grant money OK

Me: Take it from me: DON'T OPEN A PET SOCK FACTORY. Nothing but headaches. A friend suggested I open a shoe factory for pets. Whoever saw a dog wearing boots. Give me a break.

FF: Please take care of that, there is a lot of bad people out there ok

Me: I've texted them directly and told them to ignore my kids. They were drunk from the huge party last night and hallucinating. The Secret Service agent said they will have a sheriff call me later. I wonder why?

FF: Juts text the number I send to you now and let them know you are ready to claim your grant money Ok

Me: No money for the agent. Can you believe the *#%$ told me he wanted in and wanted his cut to stay quiet????

FF: Iyalayae

(I'm not sure, but I think our conversation is causing a stroke.)

Me: Can you send me the number again. I sent a text to the number you gave me but I got a reply back saying they didn't provide grant money. They wanted to know my CIA code word. You're not trying to get me in trouble with the Federal Government, are you?

(+12532******)

Me: I know you're still mad about me borrowing all your Tupperware and not returning it yet. I thought you'd forgiven me for it. I'd give it back, but I've got frozen chili in the big one and banana pudding in all the small ones we aren't ready to eat it yet. Thanks. I'll try again

FF: Ok

Me: I got the middle number wrong.

FF: I we be right here, So let me know what you find out OK

Me: I'm really excited. I might also buy a new car. I'm still driving the old yellow Yugo I bought with my first paycheck working at Charlie Chipper's Hipper Flippers. Talk about burger joint needing a new name. Every night I smelled like onions and old people. Come to think of it. Now I'm kind of old. And now I'm hungry. Do you want me to send you a finder's fee for helping me get the money?

FF: I'm happy to do so. You've been great. Just try the number and let me know what they told you

Me: Will do. I need a moment to help one of the kids. They have to take Latin, translate it into French, then speak it in Spanish. This new Foreign Language High School means business. It doesn't help the only foreign language I know is Russian. From the time we went to Moscow on the thing. Remember? Dear Lord. Good thing I brought bail money or you'd still be there. I'd be calling you, "Comrade." Not really funny, I know, but still....You did deserve it. Is this an overseas number? There are a lot of digits.

FF: Count your own number and see if it's real or not. That was the claiming agent that I contact to get my reward claim from them OK

Me: I'm not allowed to call overseas since I got caught sneaking bananas into Japan. Part of the plea deal.

FF: It's okay then

Me: they called me a Fruit Pirate. Can you imagine??? Whoever heard of such a thing.

FF: I don't have much to say agai?????

Me: Well, if it worked for you, I'll try it. Can I ask you a quick question?

FF: What?

Me: Do you like clowns? I've learned something over the weekend and I don't know what to do about it.

FF: Not really

Me: I don't either. And I overheard a conversation at a party and one of the guys admitted to killing a clown and burying them in Lima Ohio with a unicycle and his clown outfit. I know I should call the cops, but I don't like clowns. What would you do?

FF: Don't know

Me: I don't either. tough call. OK, I'm sending the text. (Amazing the scammers don't like clowns.)

FF: Oh OK

Me: And he wasn't even a good clown. The guy couldn't make balloon animals to save his life. Literally. To. Save. His. Life.

FF: I wish you the best of luck and god bless Ok

(Nice they offered me a God Bless after talking about murder.)

Me: Thank you. Would you like a postcard from Disney Land Syria?

FF: What post card is that

Me: With the extra money we get, I'm taking the kids to Disney Land in Syria. Shorter lines. And I won't ever forget this. My wife is due to give birth. I will insist we name the boy after you. Even though you're a girl. A girl's name will help him to grow up tough. Granted, there will be lots of fights. Hey. Do you think they can send it to me in cash? Small untraceable bills? OH. WAIT. You said they deliver to your door????

FF: Yes they did. Have you text them yet???

Me: I can't have them come to the door. If I'm not home, it could be a disaster. We have those Shetland guard ponies. They are trained to hoof to death anyone they don't know. We kind of live off the grid. I've never told you about it. Sorry. They used to belong to the dead clown. We retrained them. Better than guard dogs because you can ride them when you want to. As longs as you have short legs. Can I have the money sent to you???

FF: What money Yes

Me: The grant money, silly. Cool. I still have your address from when I needed to send you the box of fire ants. I bet your ex-husband loved waking up to those.

FF: Did you text them?

Me: I've sent the text and I've got to take the kids to school. I'll let you know what I learn. Do you speak Latin, French or Spanish by any chance? They have a verb to conjugate and I don't know how to do it. I'm not sure what conjugate means. I think it's a fence you build for prisoners who misuse a foreign language. But I'm only guessing. If you can, the word is bazinga. Have a great day!

The account is now closed...

* * *

Pointing to a spot on my face, the twins asked me what happened.

Me: I got attacked by an angry woodpecker. He won.

Katy: Is this another cat story?

Me: No. It's a woodpecker story.

Lauren: What really happened?

Me: (pause) I threw a pencil at the wall and it hit eraser first, bounced off the wall and struck me in the face.

Katy: Is this another cat story?

Me: No. It's a pencil story.

Lauren: What really happened?

Me: (pause) It's a pimple.

Both girls: Go with the woodpecker story.

* * *

Overheard:

"The three of them made quite a duo."

* * *

Lauren's Fitbit wasn't synching to her new phone which necessitated a chat with one of their help people. The following conversation occurred:

Me: Seems to be taking a long time, but I will see what happens.

Byron HS: It's fine. In the meantime, is there any other request, I may assist you with? By the way, after our chat you will receive a brief survey. Any feedback you'd like to provide would be most appreciated, and will help us refine our Support processes.

Me: I'd be happy to. No Fitbit questions. I've always wondered if Paul McCartney was really the walrus. Or why my sixth grade girlfriend broke up with me, but otherwise, I'm good.

Byron HS: Oh, good questions! We are happy to assist you. You are free to end the session, take care, we'll be here when you need us.

Me: Thanks. If you find the answers to those other questions, hit me up.

Byron HS: I will! Count on that! (We shall see...)

Lauren to me: You're just like Scooby-do.

Me: Hard to argue. I do love snacks.

* * *

Discussing the start of a new school year at the dinner table:

Lauren: Please don't embarrass us again each morning when you drop us off at school like you did last year.

Me: Remember all those times you peed on me when you were three months old?

Lauren: No.

Me: I do. Payback.

Lauren: But I couldn't help it!

Me: Neither can I.

Lauren: *sigh*

* * *

Another friend got their messenger account stolen. So you know what that means. I don't know how I'm not on a list somewhere. Maybe I am, but maybe they like me.

FB Friend: Hello

Me: Howdy.

FB Friend: How are you doing today

Me: Living the dream. You?

FB Friend: Good

Me: Fantastic.

FB Friend: Have you heard about the good news?

Me: **No. Tell me more.** I could use some good news.

FB Friend: It is all about the Small Business Administration (SBA) Assistance program.

Me: I could use the help since I lost my business and I've been living in a tent for six months and the zipper is broke. And it's missing one of the poles. It's kind of breezy. I still have $10,000 stashed in case of emergencies though.

(You have to make them think you have at least a FEW dollars.)

FB Friend: It is a money grant program and is donated to randomly selected people by the Small Business Administration to assist people financially. It is for the retired and the working. Did you get yours?

Me: I would not be living in a tent if I did. I bet everything I own on a revival of pet rocks. Have you ever tried to train a rock? It doesn't go very well.

FB Friend: No

Me: And don't try it. I now have 1000 rocks that do nothing but play dead. And sit. Like all the time.

FB Friend: Okay When the FedEx men came to deliver my grant, I saw your name and picture on their list

Me: You have always been kind to me. Thank you for your friendship. That time you gave me your used bubblegum meant the world to me. Dry mouth sucks.

FB Friend: Should i give you the agent text number so that you can claim your winning?

Me: Do you think they will deliver to my tent? It is easy to find because it is yellow and it is right next to all my rocks. I used them to make ancient symbols. Except I don't speak ancient people stuff. So, I had to guess. Turned out to look more like Calvin and Hobbs. I LOVE Calvin and Hobbs. Tell them to look out for the ticked off skunk. It snuck into my tent while I was sleeping and I grabbed it thinking it was my pillow. I don't smell so good now. You would do that for me???? I'd love their number

FB Friend: Why not you will just pay for shipping and fill a short form so that they can locate you

Me: Will do. Can you fill out the form for me? I don't write so good since the accident. I'm talking to you with voice to text.

FB Friend: Yes but you will first talk to agent

Me: I was playing Frisbee golf and got my hand caught in a hornet's nest instead of a hole in one. I got stung like a billion times. Now I throw rocks at them. Give me their name and number. I will have my friend Rupert give them a call.

(I plan to make Rupert, my invisible friend, famous.)

FB Friend: +12707****** that is the agent text number

Me: Sweet. Do you think I will get enough money to buy a bigger tent?

FB Friend: Yes

Me: I have been living here with my seven pet pigs. It is very crowded. And I keep dreaming of bacon.

FB Friend: She is online now attending to some winning now

Me: I do like to win. The last time I won anything

was when I took second place at the Hells Angels motorcycle festival cake bake off. I don't eat cake anymore. The winner made a Devil's food cake. I made an angel food cake. I thought I had it in the bag. Dang Hell's Angels.

FB Friend: Call the agent now to claim your winning

Me: What is the agent's name? Do you think she will be my friend? I could use another friend. Is her name Lovenda? I love that name.

(I have a friend named Lovenda and think it's a cool name.)

FB Friend: Agent amaliavan-1

(Sounds like a hair regeneration product.)

Me: I had a sister with the name close to that. Her name is Mary. Oh no! I have a real problem. I buried my money under one of my pet rocks and now the rock is gone along with all my money. I think one of my rocks stole all my cash. Can I get the other cash soon??!

FB Friend: You are sick Me are you kidding me am trying to help you are saying rubbish

(A scammer accuses me of speaking rubbish. Ironic, no?)

Me: I am desperate. I need to get my nose whistle fixed. I beg your pardon! My problems are real. You know about all this stuff. I got the problems with the imaginary friends fixed. Mostly.

FB Friend: Call the agent i don't have time for all this

Me: I'm beginning to think you're not who you say you are. Can I trust you?

FB Friend: Yes am karen

(Am not.)

Me: Then prove it. Answer one question. Do you like clowns?

FB Friend: Do you think I could stood you so low for a scam?

Me: Answer the question please do you like clowns????

FB Friend: Yes

Me: Thank goodness. It is you. They still scare me but you've always loved them. I think it's the noses. I want to squeeze them.

FB Friend: I can't do you what will harm you

Me: Thank you. You have always been a great friend. Stop by and see me sometime. The skunk smell is getting better

FB Friend: Okay no problem

At this point my friend got wise to the problem and it was shut down.

* * *

One of the twins favorite books when they were toddlers was the story of Humpty Dumpty. We had a gorgeous book with a full picture of Humpty on the cover. One warm summer day we pulled into the drive-thru at the dry cleaners. A large woman came to the window wearing a head band which pulled back her hair from her round face and exposed a high forehead. When she opened the passenger side door to put in our clothes the following happened.

Katy: (From the back of the backseat, with awe in her voice) HUMP-TY DUMP-TY!!!

Clerk: What was that, baby?

Me: (Katy and Lauren both started to answer when I spoke over them.) Nothing. They're talking about a book. See ya.

She waved to the girls and I was quickly off.

* * *

Florida church sign:

To whoever stole my air conditioners, you are going to need them - God

* * *

THIS POST HAS A HUGE SPOILER ABOUT THE MOVIE *ROGUE ONE.*

Last night the twins and I joined the Monroe family to go see *Rogue One*. In the car on the way home, the following conversation ensued.

Me: How did you girls like the movie?

Lauren: I loved it. Can we see it in 3D?

Katy: I hated it! (She has tears in her eyes.)

Me: Why did you hate it?

Katy: (Throws her hands up in the air.) Because they all frickin' die.

Me: But they did so to save everyone else.

Katy: They still frickin' die.

Lauren: They're heroes. And their souls will continue with the force.

Katy: Frickin' die.

Me: They are like American soldiers who sacrifice their lives to protect the rest of us.

Katy: Frickin' die, frickin' die, frickin' die!

Me: Want to see it again?

Katy: Yes.

* * *

After a deer walked in front of us on the way to school:

Katy: I wish deer were really smart so they wouldn't do that.

Me: If that happened, then there might be human hunting season instead of deer hunting season.

Katy: (Momentary blank stare.) Well. Ok. Not THAT smart.

Me: You mean maybe as smart as a middle schooler? (She is in seventh grade.)

Katy: Yes. Exactly. (pauses) Hey. Wait a minute...

Me: *snicker*

* * *

At a Lowe's here in town.

Me: I'd like to buy a barrow.

Clerk: You mean a wheelbarrow? They're over this way. (We start walking.)

Me: No. Just a barrow. No wheel needed.

Clerk: I'm sorry. They all come with wheels.

Me: When they have a wheel, they are wheelbarrows. I want a simple barrow. No wheel needed.

Clerk: Why don't you want the wheel?

Me: Because I have the strength of ten men. And I'm trying to lose weight. I think carrying around the barrow instead of wheeling it around, will be better exercise.

Clerk: (Gives me the "you're seriously crazy" look.) I don't think you're THAT strong, and while I get you wanting to lose weight, I think ending up in the hospital won't help you.

Me: Depends on how cute the nurses are.

(We reach the wheelbarrows.)

Clerk: I guess you can take off one of the wheels. If you really wanted to.

Me: (I point to one) I'll take that one. Can you load it into my Rogue?

Clerk: What happened to the strength of ten men?

Me: I don't want to peak too early.

Clerk: *sigh*

* * *

On Father's Day the girls made me a card that said I'm the BDE because I kill spiders, help them with homework, I scare off creepy people, drive them around (that's an understatement), give good advise (so they think), put up with their crap (true), and I'm a human ATM (very true).

Katy: You're the Best Dad Ever.

Me: YES I AM!

Katy: Gloat much?

Me: All the time.

Katy: Would the best dad ever really do that?

Me: Is this a trick question?

Katy: *sigh*

* * *

The twins and I went to Tumbleweed one night and it was buy one burrito dinner, get one free. Katy ordered chicken fingers, and Lauren ordered a burrito dinner. Then the following conversation happened.

Waitress: And you sir?

Me: I'll have the burrito dinner with a salad and baked potato as my sides, and please hold the burrito.

Waitress: So you only want to order a salad and potato?

Me: No. I want the burrito dinner with a salad and baked potato, hold the burrito.

(Waitress shoots me "the look.")

Waitress: That's not a burrito dinner.

Me: I could have you fix the full meal, then not eat the burrito. Or you can hold the burrito and save on food costs.

Waitress: (raised eyebrow) Burrito dinner, hold the burrito. Got it.

She held the burrito.

* * *

I came home to find water on the floor in the kitchen. No obvious source. Cleaned it up. Wife came home. Found more water on the floor. Thought it might have come from the ceiling. I was with Katy at her basketball tournament. Wife calls the plumber, Steven Miller, to come over straight away to find and fix the problem.

Wife: (Calls) Well, we found the problem.

Me: Give me the bad news.

(I'm picturing walls torn up, pipes ripped out, kitchen ceiling repairs)

Wife: It was in the pantry.

Me: (Confused) We don't have any plumbing in the pantry.

Wife: No, but we do have a gallon of spring water that leaked.

Me: How hard is the plumber laughing?

Wife: He knows you. Figures it's normal around here.

Me: *sigh*

* * *

Back in 2002 I lost a hundred pounds. (Then I

became a stay at home dad and lost all my good habits.) I went to the Y and after 10 minutes on an elliptical machine I was dying. Then this short skinny guy on the elliptical next to me spoke up.

Short Skinny Guy: You know, I used to be just like you.

Me: What? Fat?

Short Skinny Guy: No. Slow.

Me: If I wasn't so tired, I'd get off this machine, take a nap, then chase your butt down and sit on you.

Short Skinny Guy: You'd never catch me.

Me: Maybe not, but I'll find your house and eat all your food.

Short Skinny Guy: That's just mean.

Me: *sigh*

* * *

Another trick-r-treat story, sort of:

Lauren: Dad, did you go trick-r-treating in the olden days?

Me: Yes, but we lived in the country so we had to trick or treat the cows.

Lauren: Did they give you milk?

Me: Yes, that and cow puckey.

Lauren: (after very long pause) I think I would rather just have the milk.

* * *

Here we go again. FF is Facebook Friend.

FF: Hello, how are you?

Me: Doing well. Working on my Pulitzer Prize. And you?

FF: I'm good, enjoying the moment of life and how is life treating you?

Me: I can't complain. But I will. I hate lima beans.

FF: Good, hope you have heard of New USA grants??

Me: **No. Tell me more.**

FF: The program is specially placed for those who need assistance paying for bills, starting their own business, helping raise their children with old and retired people or even buying a new home. Have you heard of them?

Me: No. But you can't believe how much I need the loan. I've almost run out of money.

FF: I applied before getting the money and I was told I was eligible to receive the grant money and I got $200,000 from them, delivered to me while you don't have to pay it back.

Me: OH MY GOODNESS!!! Think I can get that amount?

FF: You can apply for it too.

Me: I'm building a miniature version of the Sistine Chapel here in Goshen and I'm broke. It's about 1/250 the size of the real thing. I loved what Michelangelo did and wanted to recreate it. Chapels are expensive. How do I apply?

FF: Should I share the agent link?

Me: If that's how I do it. You know he painted the ceiling while lying on his back? I tried that and ended up with paint all over me. I got it in my eyes and it almost blinded me. How do I reach the agent?

(She gives me a name and phone number.)

Me: The other problem is he had a ton of different paints. I only have blue, white and a blotch of yellow. And he used brushes. I only have paint rollers. Can you hang on a sec? The preacher who I hired to do sermons at the chapel is here.

FF: That is the agent link you will message him that you also wot to apply or it too (Yeah, I don't get it either.)

Me: Sweet. I tried to paint the mural where God and Man touch fingers, but mine looks like Gumby and a skinny Santa trying to thumb wrestle.

FF: Click their facebook page, like it and then call this number 989-262-0866.

Me: The agent looks like a stamp collector I once knew. He died from licking too much of the glue on the back of the stamps. He licked them all the time. It was sad.

FF: They delivered mine at my mail box in check cause that was what I applied for.

Me: It will be one more second. The minister is really mad at me. Evidently my Sistine Chapel looks like the outside of a discotheque. He's not happy with me but I had blurry pictures of the Sistine Chapel and I couldn't really tell.

FF: Ok do that now and get back to me so I can tell you what to do next.

Me: Sweet. I may need to leave the country. The minister just called me a clown. Do you like clowns?

(I love to see what the scammers think of clowns. You would think they would be warned: if the guy asks about clowns, stop talking. Guess not)

FF: So did you try it?

Me: Not yet. I'm still arguing with the preacher. Now he's trying to convert me. He's a minister of Kanardism. They don't believe in science.

(The twins had a teacher, Mr. Kanard, who joked today he didn't believe in science. It might take off.)

FF: Okay you can keep me posted.

Me: You never answered my question. Do you believe in clowns?

FF: What did you mean by saying that. Are you cursing me?

(Never knew clowns were a curse word. Wonder what country they live in?)

Me: Cursing. I simply asked if you liked clowns.

FF: No

Me: Me either. I think they are scary. Then they become politicians. Can I get my money in cash?

FF: I got my money delivered.

Me: I owe a lot of money for the paint and I'm worried they'll come looking for me. Think it's ok to build a chapel and then hide the money? Kanardism says it's not a good thing.

FF: You can try and contact the agent now.

Me: The minister just left. I can call in a bit. I'm charging up my phone. I ran the battery down filming all the ducks walking through the chapel. I heard they were good luck. Not really. They ate all the hymnals.

(Long pause. I guess they were thinking about ducks.)

Me: Are you still there?

FF: Yes.

Me: Thank goodness. I know you've been in poor health since the accident where you were injured by the ice cream truck. Ironic you don't like ice cream. Hmmm...I must have called the wrong number. A woman answered and she was speaking Chinese. Did you give me the wrong number on purpose?

FF: Did you call the agent I gave you? Like their facebook page then message them.

Me: I called the number you gave me. I think I just accidentally ordered 100 stuffed teddy bears. Now I have NO money.

FF: Have you sent the message?

Me: I think you are playing a joke on me. Did my dad put you up to this?

FF: No.

Me: He's been mad at me since I sold his Slim Whitman album collection. I don't know why he's so mad. I bought him three new pairs of lederhosen. He's been fired up since he found out we were 1/365th German. We are also part Bartswanistanikstan. Weird, huh?

FF: I don't understand what you are saying.

(I get this from non-scammers, too.)

Me: I'll try the number again. Do you need any teddy bears? I have a bunch of them coming. I might see if my friend Opus needs them.

(Bloom County fans will get this one.)

FF: No.

Me: Did you hear I won the latest round of Who Wants to be an Auctioneer? Turns out I talk really fast. I'm excited about the money.

FF: Did you contact the agent? They are waiting to hear from you.

Me: I'm on hold. I think this one is right. They asked me if I'd be willing to give them my SSN and other information. I said, Heck yeah for 200 grand.

FF: Please let me know when you are finished.

Me: That's weird. They want to know my zodiac sign. When I told the guy I was a Capricorn, they laughed at me and put me back on hold. I like the elevator music they're playing. I think it's Boxcar Willy. What a singer. Sold more albums than the Beatles.

FF: Ok.

Me: I'm going to have to use messenger. They want my high school transcripts. Because it's a government loan, they want to know what grade I got in Civics. I got all As by the way.

(I think that's actually right.)

At this point, they disabled the scammer account.

* * *

When asked who was singing a song on the radio:

Me: Sir Paul McCartney of the Beatles.

Lauren: Hey dad, you may not know this, but they broke up.

Me: Thanks Pumpkin. I'm slow on my 1970's band break up news.

* * *

In line at McDonalds drive-thru after ordering a diet Dr. Pepper, to the clerk with the line not moving:

Me: I bet the guy up front ordered something really strange, like a Filet McMuffin.

Clerk: A what?

Me: A Filet McMuffin. It's where you order a Filet O Fish but put it on an English muffin of an Egg McMuffin.

Clerk: Who would ever order that?

(I get out a five-dollar bill and hand it to her.)

Clerk: You can't be serious?

Me: I am a paragon of seriousness.

Clerk: A para what?

Me: Paragon of—it means I'm serious.

Clerk: (shakes her head and places the order). After a pause she says into her headset: Yes. That's right. Yes. He's serious.

Me: A paragon of seriousness.

Clerk: (hands me my change.) You're something alright.

Me: Thank you.

* * *

One day we picked up a dog for a client and the following conversation took place.

Lauren: How old is the dog?

Me: 7 and a half, I think.

Lauren: How much is that in human years?

Me: Same age as me, around 52.

Lauren: Oh. So you're really old then?

Me: (Raised eyebrow.)

Lauren: Let me guess. Another hit to my college fund?

Me: Smart kid.

* * *

Every year we host a large Christmas party for our friends. When the twins were about 6, Santa Claus stopped by for a visit. All the kids started yelling Santa's name when he walked in the door.

Katy waited impatiently on the steps in anticipation to greet Santa with this year's special request.

Katy: Santa, Santa, Santa! (She finally yelled above the other children) I want a REAL hamster this year, not of the fake ones.

(Zhu Zhu pets were THE difficult gift to find that Christmas season.)

Santa: Well, Katy, I haven't delivered live animals since the 1070s.

Katy: (Hands on her hips) I've been VERY good this year.

Santa: I know you have honey, but it's not fair to have live animals riding in my sack all night.

Katy: (Not happy at all, throws her hands up in the air) Whatever.

(Then she stormed off. I followed her into the family room where she now sat, pouting and sitting with her arms crossed.)

Me: You do realize you just blew off Santa Claus—with Christmas less than two week away. Are you sure that's a good idea?

Katy: Fine. I'll go talk to him.

(By this time Santa was in the living room and kids were taking turns sitting on his lap, excitedly telling him what they wanted for Christmas. Katy was the last one to take a turn.)

Santa: You've grown so much this year. You're doing well in school. I'm so proud of you. ("Our" Santa is so good with the kids.) So what would you like for Christmas, Katy?

Katy: (Heavy sigh, still pouting) If I can't have a REAL hamster, I'll take a fake one.

Me: (Santa glanced my way and I mouthed) *I have two.*

Santa: (Santa nodded sagely) Since you and your

sister Lauren have been especially good this year, I'll bring you both one.

Another parent: (Whispered in my ear) Is he nuts? He's promising you'll get two Zhu Zhu pets. You're hosed.

Me: (Laughed) and told her not to worry.

Turns out I'd lucked into getting two of them while at Toys R Us—I only got them because there was a frenzy when they were put on the shelf right in front of me. I'd never even heard of the things.

Katy went away happy and Christmas was saved.

* * *

One day the twins and I were trading jokes and then I stumped them.

Me: What's the difference between an orange?

Lauren: Between an orange and what?

Me: That's all I can tell you.

Katy: That makes no sense. There has to be more.

Me: There's not.

(The girls trade answers, but they are all wrong.)

Lauren: What's the answer then?

Me: It's a motorcycle because a telephone post doesn't have doors.

(The twins stare at me a long time.)

Katy: That makes NO sense at all.

Me: Now you get it.

Lauren: No we don't.

Me: Yes you do.

(This is a nonsense joke. We used to tell them back in our day.)

Twins: *sigh*

* * *

Cracker Barrel waitress: Can I get you anything else?

Me: Do you have any Peace on Earth, Goodwill towards men?

Waitress: We sure don't, but we do have pecan pie.

Me: That works.

ACKNOWLEDGMENTS

First I would like to thank all of my friends on Facebook who encouraged me to gather my funny conversations into one collection. Knowing I've been able to bring laughter into other's daily lives is a wonderful thing.

I would also like to thank my family, my wife Karin and twins Katy and Lauren, who must suffer my attempts at humor on an almost minute by minute basis. I am not always as funny as I think I am and they make sure to keep the laugh track going even when I'm not.

And finally I would like to thank all the store clerks out there who have interacted with me over the years. Your willingness to put up with me and not call the authorities is much appreciated.

ABOUT THE AUTHOR

Award winning author, publisher and screenwriter, Tony Acree, likes putting characters in situations they think they will never survive, and find out if they're right. He lives near Louisville, Kentucky with his wife, twin daughters, two female dogs, two female cats, and says the way the goldfish looks at him, he's sure she's female, too.

He is also the publisher of the award winning small press, Hydra Publications. You can email him at Tonyacree@gmail.com

ALSO BY TONY ACREE

The Victor McCain Thrillers

The Hand of God

The Watchers

The Speaker

Revenge

The Samantha Tyler Thrillers

Vengeance: A Samantha Tyler Thriller cowritten by Rachael Rawlings

Victor McCain Short Stories

Nightmare

Back to Hell

Lonnie, The Hand of God and Me cowritten by Marian Allen

www.ingramcontent.com/pod-product-compliance
Lightning Source LLC
Chambersburg PA
CBHW031629040426
42452CB00007B/751